Foulridge Methodist
Sunday School

Presented to

Steven Booth

1976

PICKERING & INGLIS LTD. PRINTED IN GREAT BRITAIN

THE PUDDY STONE

MR BUMP

THE PUDDY STONE

by
KIM SIMMONS

VICTORY PRESS
EASTBOURNE

ISBN 0 85476 223 X

Printed in Great Britain for
VICTORY PRESS (Evangelical Publishers Ltd.),
Lottbridge Drove, Eastbourne, Sussex,
by Richard Clay (The Chaucer Press) Ltd.,
Bungay, Suffolk.

CONTENTS

CHAPTER ONE

THE LEVEL-CROSSING KIDS

There were six children digging in the hummocky field. Justin saw them out of the bus window and he knew who they were—the family who had come to live in the rather ugly house by the level-crossing.

That was Carol in the green jersey, bossing everyone about as usual; little fat Kate with her red hair, and Pete who was busy doing nothing.

Justin twisted round to try to see what they were up to as the bus crawled towards the crossing gates. Mark, he noticed, was wearing red jeans with his wellington boots and that made him look like the hussar in a print Justin had in his bedroom. Sandy, the eldest, was leaning on a pickaxe. Mark was the only one working really hard, and digging as though his life depended on it, and there was a girl helping him. That girl Justin didn't know. She had sandy hair in untidy plaits, and she looked as thin and wiry as a greyhound.

The six were so absorbed in what they were doing that none of them looked up as the bus went by. Justin hadn't bothered himself much about the Ridett family since they moved into the village, but he knew there were five of them, and now there seemed to be six. Suddenly he wanted very much to join them and make a seventh.

Then the signal-box hid them from sight and he

gathered up his satchel and books. Oh, blow this homework! he thought, as the train roared through, and then the crossing gates swung open. Just for once I'm going to get up early and do most of it. Tonight I'm going to see what's happening in that field as soon as I've had my tea.

It was only too easy to decide to let the homework wait. For one thing it was Friday, so it would only mean taking a chunk out of Saturday morning. For another it was history, which he hated, and the early Britons, which was worse. Definitely it was a chore to be avoided as long as possible.

He hurried down the road from the bus stop, swinging his case and feeling the spring wind warm on his face for a change. It was nice to know that winter was out of the way and there was a long, light evening ahead.

He let himself into the bungalow and went to open the windows and feel the warm wind blow through. His meal was set ready as usual. He lifted up the covering plate and saw with satisfaction a slice of pie in a circle of tomato and lettuce.

"Good," said Justin to himself. "Nice quick grub and no washing-up to speak of. I'll be down the road again in two ticks!"

Since his father died Justin got used to fending for himself a good deal. His mother was a nurse, and their companionship had to depend on her hours of duty. When she was on nights Justin slept with a kindly old couple just across the road. They gave him his breakfast and sent him off to school. But on that Friday evening his mother would be home fairly soon, so Justin left a tidy table and the kettle filled, in spite of his haste. Mum was the kind of person one was glad to do things nicely for.

As he hurried down the road towards the railway he was suddenly anxious lest The Crossing Kids should have packed up and gone away. The sunny evening would feel very flat and empty if they had.

But a few yards further on his spirits rose again. He caught a glimpse of Carol's green jersey beyond the signal-box, and saw with joy that the gates were open. Two minutes later he strolled on to the field with his hands in his pockets, trying to look as though he had just been passing and was mildly curious.

Pete saw him first and straightened up, wiping muddy hands on the seat of his jeans. "Hullo!" he said. "You're the boy from the bungalow, aren't you? You don't go to our school up the road."

"Hullo!" echoed Justin. "You all live in the house by the rail. You're Carol and Sandy and Pete and Mark and Kate. I know, because my mother's friend keeps the little shop down by the garage, and she knows everybody. Mum says she talks like a gramophone with the needle stuck. What are you doing, anyway?"

"We're doing a bit of quarrying," explained Sandy, from beyond the hole. "We want to make a rockery and a paved place, and bird-bath in our garden."

Carol added, "It's jolly hard work too."

Pete said, "You might get out a stone or two yourself, if you're not too clean. Anne here has done an awful lot, but she's just cut her thumb so she's not much use now."

The girl with the sandy plaits didn't seem to belong to the family. She stood sucking her injured thumb and watching the others as they added to the pile of broken stonework and half bricks which was growing larger minute by minute. Mark and Pete burrowed into the chalky soil and threw up their finds on to the turf.

"But how did all this get buried down here?" asked Justin, jumping down beside Pete and beginning to work out a half brick with his stubby fingers.

"Reckon there was a building of some sort here," said Sandy. "Our dad thinks it was put up when the railway was being built ages ago. Just a place for workmen to sleep and eat in, probably, but they put things up pretty solid in those days. By the time the trains were running it wasn't being used any more, so after a bit it fell down. I guess people took most of the stone away to build walls and things, and the grass grew over the rest."

For half an hour Justin worked with a will, getting his school trousers very chalky in the process. He ought to have changed, of course, before he came out, but somehow there hadn't been time. Apart from worrying a bit about what his mother would say when she saw them, he was blissfully happy. The Ridetts had accepted him so easily, and just went on with their stone quarrying as though he had been one of the team always.

"It's time we shifted some of this lot along to the garden," said Sandy at last. "It's no good getting such a mountain if we don't really need it all. You go and get the barrow, Anne; that won't hurt your thumb."

Without a word Anne went off towards the house. Justin stopped trying to dust the chalk of his trousers and watched her go.

"What is she? A cousin or something?" he asked. "I've not seen her in the village before."

"She's not generally in the village," Carol told him.

"She's not a cousin, or a school-friend, either. She's staying in the house the other side of the station while her mother's in hospital. Her aunt is a friend of Mother's, so we ask her for the evening now and then. She's all right, but awfully quiet."

"She belongs over at Stannard's Cross," said Pete, "but her dad's at sea, so they've shut the cottage up for a bit. She's ages getting that barrow," he added; "I guess she's wandered in to talk to Mother."

"I'll go and see!" volunteered Mark, promptly, and he went racing away. He was a jolly little boy who reminded Justin of a willing pony, and he seemed the first to volunteer for any job.

He appeared a minute or two later trundling the metal barrow through the gap in the hedge which served as a back entrance to the Ridetts' garden, and came with it along the narrow track that the children had worn with their comings and goings.

Anne came after him with her thumb properly bandaged.

"Mrs Ridett saw me," she said. "She asked what I'd done, so now I'm off duty for today. Don't forget that I'll need some sick pay after all the work I've put in!"

"You've got a hope," chuckled Pete, and Sandy was just going to say something cheerfully rude when Kate caught their attention.

"Come and see what I've found!" she cried. "It's a round thing with carving on it!"

The others had been standing about in the evening sunshine, resting their tired backs and stiff fingers, and waiting for the barrow, but little fat Kate had been scrabbling about in a deep hole that Sandy had made. She crouched there holding something in her grubby hand which at first glance looked like an ordinary stone.

"Let's have a look," said Sandy. "It's just a flint, I expect."

Kate handed it up, saying quickly, "You can look, but you can't keep it. I found it, and it's mine!"

"That's not just a flint!" exclaimed Justin, looking at the strange stone as Sandy turned it round. "Flints don't have neat patterns on them. Perhaps it's a bit of decoration off the building that used to be here."

The moment he had said it he knew it was a stupid idea. No one would decorate a place put up for gangers to sleep in while they made a railway line. Pete gave him a look which said as much.

Anne held out her uninjured hand. "My turn," she said. "If it's got a pattern someone must have carved it. I'd guess it's much, much older than the railway."

She took it from Sandy and turned it over, looking at the lines of dots and indentations which made a circular pattern. It had a faintly marked cross in the very centre.

"It could have been part of a row of carved stones above a door, something to make a place look special. I think it was part of a wall put up ages and ages ago." She held it so long, after rubbing some of the dirt off it on the knee of her jeans, that Kate began to get anxious.

"It's a puddy stone, and it's mine!" she said, firmly. "You give it back!"

They all turned and looked at her, even Carol, who had got bored with it and was beginning to load the barrow.

"What's that you said? How do you know what it's called? None of us ever saw one before!"

Sandy looked down at his youngest sister with

amusement, but not great surprise. Kate sometimes had gleanings of information in her young head which astonished everybody.

"It's a puddy stone," said Kate, calmly, "because it's round like my hands are when I wear my gloves that only have a thumb, in the winter. Grandma calls them 'puddy paws', and that stone looks as if it has knitting on it, so it's a puddy stone. I want it back, please."

"Trust Kate to come up with a silly answer!" Sandy turned away, and Carol heaved a big stone into the barrow. Pete went to help her and soon they were all working again. All except Anne and Kate. They were looking at the stone together and talking in whispers. It seemed to Justin, who caught a word or two as he passed by, that a bargain was being struck.

He was certain a moment later when he saw Anne pull off a rather nice chunky bangle she was wearing and hand it to small Kate. Kate seized it with delight, and the puddy stone changed hands.

The barrow was trundled to and fro a good many times from the 'quarry' to the garden. Sometimes Sandy pushed it, and sometimes Justin did, because they were the strongest. When Pete and Mark took it they kept stopping to rest, and to wave to passengers in passing trains.

Justin was really impressed by the garden that The Level-crossing Kids had devised. The half-built rockery would look splendid, he thought, when pansies and tulips, and green cushions of thrift grew there one day. They had dug a hole already for the big old sink that they found half buried in rubbish. That would be a pool for goldfish soon, and every flat stone they came across went to make a stretch of pavement round it.

All too soon the sunshine vanished and the spring evening began to feel chilly. Mrs Ridett appeared at the back door to call Kate to bath and bed. Anne left the workers and went in as well to say good-bye. Justin looked at his watch. "Time I got home, I guess," he said. "Mum will be wondering where I've got to."

"Come any time you want," invited Carol, graciously, and she added with candour, "We can do with your muscle power."

The crossing gates were shut when Justin reached them, and as he waited beside the impatient cars somebody came alongside him. It was Anne, on a ramshackle bicycle.

CHAPTER TWO

MR CASSIDY

Justin was really rather a shy person. Anne with a crowd of other people had been easy to talk to, but Anne by herself suddenly made him feel awkward. He glanced up at her as she managed a wobbly balance with one toe on the ground, and wished that she would say something first, or that the train would go roaring through.

Then, to his own surprise, he blurted out just the right thing.

"What made you think that Kate's 'puddy stone' is terribly old? How old? And who carved it?"

Anne stopped wobbling and dismounted. She pulled the stone with difficulty from the pocket of her jeans and put it on her handlebar to look at it again.

"I don't know a lot," she said, "but sometimes I have a good guess. My guess at the moment is that it's as old as Norman, or Saxon, or even older. I think only pretty early people would bother to decorate stones like this, because it's not even perfectly round. Later people would have quarried big stones and carved them."

Her voice was drowned as an express train thundered by. It vanished into the distance but the crossing gates didn't open.

"Blow!" said Justin. "That means a goods train coming the other way. You must be jolly keen on that stone to barter for it with young Kate. I'd say she has the best of the bargain."

"Oh! that bracelet? I liked it, but I've got lots of bangles; I was mad on collecting them last year. I want this stone to show to Mr Cassidy. He'll probably know some marvellous story about it."

Anne tucked the stone back in her pocket as the goods train came slowly into view. By the time it had passed, Justin had discovered that Mr Cassidy lived over at Stannard's Cross where Anne came from, and that he knew just about all there was to know concerning the early Britons and things of that sort.

Justin pricked up his ears. He was reminded unpleasantly of his homework, still crammed into the case at home. Although the subject had seemed terribly dull when he was given it, the 'puddy stone' had awakened his curiosity.

"When will you take it over?" he asked. "I've got a bike and I could come, too, if it's tomorrow. Would Mr Cassidy mind?"

"Shouldn't think so. He can be crusty sometimes, but he likes people if they're interested. I could meet you at two o'clock tomorrow by the garage. I'll have to help Aunt Madge with the dinner things first."

The gates swung back and Anne was caught in the tide of cars and cycles. She went ahead with a wave of the hand, leaving Justin to wander home, hands in pockets. It had been a good evening and suddenly it seemed as though it might be a good weekend.

His mother was talking over the fence to their next-door neighbour when he reached the bungalow, so Justin slipped un-noticed through the back way. In his room he hastily changed his trousers and gave his school ones a furious brushing. To his great relief nearly all the chalk and dried mud came off, and he folded them neatly over the back of his chair. When he clattered through to the living-room a few minutes later he had an atlas under his arm, and carried a sheaf of paper for a project. For once, he was willing to forgo television and make a start on his homework.

Justin had no touble at all in meeting Anne at two o'clock on that windy, showery Saturday. His mother wasn't working, and she gave him a specially early meal. She had listened with interest over a late breakfast to his description of The Level-crossing Kids and Kate's puddy stone.

"I know a little about Mr Cassidy," she said. "He collects all kinds of things, I believe. Ancient pottery and carvings, and Chinese jade, too. It's nice of Anne to take you."

Chinese jade! thought Justin. I hope that if Kate's stone isn't really anything special he won't be high and mighty about it.

Suddenly he knew that he would hate to see Anne snubbed.

She was already waiting beside the crossing gate when he cycled up. "Thought I'd save you coming to the garage," she called, and added, "I'm glad none of the Ridetts has spotted me—Sandy or Carol would be sure to want to come as well, and Mr Cassidy isn't keen on masses of children all at once."

"Guess they've gone out for the day," said Justin, as they bumped over the rails, but all the same they rode extra fast till they were out of sight of the house beside the line.

The way to Stannard's Cross was through winding lanes, with glimpses of the sea now and then where chalky fields sloped towards the shore. The railway ran between them and the water all the way, much to Anne's disgust. "It spoils the picture," she said, "though it isn't as bad as power-lines and pylons. I'm glad we can't see it from our cottage, anyway."

Justin had cycled over to Stannard's Cross once or twice before. He liked the white-painted, wooden cottages and the oast houses that stood up behind the farm. He liked Anne's cottage, too, when she pointed it out—a low place with flinty walls and little dormer windows in its roof, which gave it a jaunty air. The garden, he noticed, was full of daffodils.

"We can pick some on the way back," Anne told him. "Your mother might like some."

Mr Cassidy's house stood at the top of the village. It was a rambling old place almost choked by the jasmine and roses which climbed to the upper windows, and darkened by a great yew tree which leaned over the churchyard wall.

They left their cycles beside the gate, and Anne went to tug the ancient bell-pull which hung by the door. Mr Cassidy was a long time coming, and when he did he looked at them over the tops of his glasses with a scarcely welcoming air.

He didn't say Good afternoon, or Come in; he just stood there. Justin found it rather disconcerting.

"We haven't come to bother you," said Anne boldly. "We won't come in if you're busy, but I've brought something to show you."

"All right. Go in and amuse yourselves in the gallery. I won't be long. Don't touch things, young man. Anne knows the way."

He stood back to let them pass, and Anne gave Justin a little push, as though to say 'so far so good'.

She went down a narrow passage which had a glass door at the end of it giving a glimpse of a large garden beyond. There was another door, and she pushed it open. Justin stood quite still for a moment, wide-eyed with surprise.

They were in a long, narrow room which had windows all down one side looking out over the garden. The opposite wall was covered with pictures and prints, and below them, and along under the windows, were glass-topped cases. Shelves filled the wall at the far end, and on them were jars, plates and tankards, and carvings of every kind.

"Wow!" said Justin. "What a place! D'you know what half of the things are?"

"Just about half!" chuckled Anne. "Most of them are labelled or I'd never remember."

For several minutes neither of them spoke. Justin leaned over the glass cases gazing at medals and coins, army badges and ancient keys, and wondered how long it had taken to gather them all together. Then he stopped by a case which he found most puzzling. It had a neat label stuck to the woodwork which said simply, 'Steps to God'.

"Steps to God!" echoed Justin, and he stood frowning a little as he tried to make sense of it. In front of the case was a very old, tattered copy of *The Pilgrim's Progress,* opened to show the quaint woodcut illustrations on pages brown with age. Well, that was about someone called Christian, he knew, but the other things were not so easy. There was a queer square thing which looked like bone, and had the alphabet carved on it, and a little cross at the top corner in faded red. There was a small piece of parchment with words he couldn't read at all, but with so much decoration in gold and red and blue that it glowed like a jewel. There was a long chip of something that looked like a broken plant pot and had a fish drawn on it, and there was a slab of stone with a cross beautifully carved. Strap-like lines twisted round it and over it in a basketwork pattern, and even Justin could tell that it was very, very old.

Anne was busy at the far end of the room looking at the people and boats on a piece of Chinese ivory, and she was quite startled when Justin cried out suddenly, "Look! Oh, look! There's another one!"

He was pointing to the corner of the glass case, and there, half hidden by a beautifully worked sampler of the Lord's Prayer, was a 'puddy stone'.

"Funny—I've looked at this case heaps of times and I've never noticed that before!" Anne longed to lift up the glass and take a closer look, but she knew better than to touch any of old Mr Cassidy's treasures unless he was there. She pulled out her own stone and set it on the wooden rim. It was larger than the one in the case, but the pattern was not so strongly marked.

"So it *is* a special thing of some sort!" she said, with pleasure, and just then they heard steps along the passage.

"Oh! Mr Cassidy! You've got what I came to bring you, already!" Anne turned to him, flushed and bright-eyed, and even Justin forgot to be shy.

"Did you dig that little stone out of a field? And why is it a step to God?" he asked. "I used not to like museums, but this is great!"

"What little stone? Oh, that in the corner. Did you say you have brought me one?"

Mr Cassidy looked surprised, but pleased as well, and Anne hastened to say, "Brought it to show you, I mean. Not to give you, unless you want it terribly badly."

She held out Kate's barter, and Mr Cassidy took it in his thin old fingers and turned it over. "A nice one," he murmured, "a very nice one. Where did you find it?"

Anne explained about The Level-crossing Kids and their 'stone quarry', and the old man grunted with approval. Justin hoped very much that Anne was going to get her stone back, and that it wouldn't just join the other one in the glass case.

"But who carved it?" he asked. "Sandy thought it was a bit of decoration from the railwaymen's hut, but Anne thinks it's older than Norman."

Mr Cassidy chuckled. "Very much older," he told them. "In fact it's millions of years old. Nobody carved it except nature. It's the imprint of a fossil on a stone—the skeleton of a little sea-creature pressed into the mud which has turned into stone uncounted years ago. The old Kentish name for it is a 'shepherd's kiss'."

"A shepherd's kiss!" echoed Anne. "That sounds pretty silly. Whatever had they to do with shepherds?"

Mr Cassidy went to sit on a high-backed chair by the window. "In old times," he told them, "it was mostly shepherds who found these patterned stones. They had lonely days on the downs and plenty of time to look around them. Farm lads sometimes saw them, too, in those flinty fields which make us wonder how they ever got ploughed. Because they looked unusual they were used as love tokens. When a tongue-tied young man didn't know how to propose to a girl of his choice he would present her with one of these, and she would know what he meant. Of course, all the shy young men didn't have them to give. You might hunt for a year or two and never see one, and they'd seldom be as evenly marked as this."

"So it really is a kind of treasure?" cried Anne, but Justin was still puzzled. "But why is there one in the case marked, 'Steps to God'?" he asked, and went back to look at the things set out under the glass.

"I put it there," said Mr Cassidy, "because long, long ago, when the people of England first became Christians, they thought, like you did, that the stones had been carved by man. They had no idea who could have done it, but because many stones had a pattern like a cross in the centre they regarded them as blessed things. They treasured them in the days when common people had very few treasures. I count my small stone as one of the earliest steps to God because surely anything that makes one think of Him brings a blessing. To the pagans, who had learned a little of our faith from Augustine, one of these was a wonderful thing to find."

Anne and Justin stayed quite a while longer, learning how the square with the alphabet on it was a child's 'horn book' three hundred years ago. How the red cross in the corner was to remind them to ask God's blessing on their work. The shard with the fish on it was a token which one Christian could give another in the days when Christians had to worship in secret, Mr Cassidy told them, because the fish was a kind of 'password' meaning 'Jesus'.

Justin leaned his elbows on the glass, and for the first time he felt that knowing about the past wasn't dull. In fact it was exciting. Those things in the case had been handled by real people, boys like himself, and girls like Anne.

"If each one could tell their own story," he said, half to himself, "wouldn't it be splendid!"

In his mind he was seeing a little dark man in a coat of skins who had first come upon Kate's puddy stone.

CHAPTER THREE

OPERATION PROPELLER

The rest of the afternoon was very good indeed. Mr Cassidy gave Anne back her stone, and, to their great delight, he opened a drawer and took out a bag of tiny coins. He poured some into his palm and stirred them about with one long finger before he picked out two of the largest.

"One for each of you," he said. "They're Roman, dug up half a mile from here. Put them somewhere safe and add to them as the years go by and you find old things that interest you. A collector never gets bored, you know, and collecting is a fine way of making friends."

He dismissed them as abruptly as he had greeted them, but they went to fetch their cycles knowing that he had been pleased with their visit.

"What now?" asked Justin. "Mother said you could come back and have some tea if you'd like to. When I get home I'll have to find a very special box to put my coin in."

"Daffodils first," said Anne. "You can pick an armful for your mother while I open the cottage and see if there's any letters. I guess I'd better be over here for a bit tomorrow and have the doors and windows open; it usually smells awfully shut-up when I come. I could go to church in the evening for a change; Auntie wouldn't mind."

So they went to the flint cottage, and Justin prowled round the rather neglected garden till Anne joined him with a handful of letters and bills. Then they cycled back easily with the wind behind them, talking about Mr Cassidy and all the people who had lived long ago around the few square miles they knew best.

"You'll be able to tell young Kate what her 'puddy stone' really is," said Justin. "She'll probably be disappointed. I guess she imagines some little man carving it."

"So did we," Anne reminded him bluntly. "I'd like to find one myself one day. Depending on what sort of pattern it had, I'd call it a 'shepherd's kiss' or a 'step to God'."

Justin's mother liked Anne very much, and Anne enjoyed her tea and Justin's record-player till it was nearly supper time.

"I'd better get back," she said, rather guiltily. "Aunt Madge will be getting bothered. I shan't be stopping to tell Kate what her stone is tonight!"

Justin watched her ride away down the lane and then went to his room whistling. It had been a good day.

Sunday usually felt pretty blank if his mother wasn't at home, but when Justin woke up the next morning he was still feeling cheerful. His mother was on early duty at the hospital, so he cooked himself breakfast and wondered what The Level-crossing Kids did on Sundays. He was just making up his mind to find out, when another idea came to him. The sun was out, and the wind wasn't as boisterous as it had been, so it was just the right day to go searching for a puddy stone of his own.

He guessed that the flinty fields which sloped towards the railway line and the sea would be the place to find one, and that, if he took his mother's garden trowel to dig around with, it might be a help.

Suppose I find one before Anne does! he thought with a chuckle. Anne, he remembered, was going to cycle back to her empty home to let some sunshine in. Then he remembered something else. 'I could go to church in the evening for a change,' Anne had said, and that surprised him.

Going to church, except when his mother took him at Christmas and Easter, was a waste of time, Justin considered. What was the point, anyway? But if a sensible girl like Anne wanted to go, then there might be something in it after all. Justin frowned as he washed up his few breakfast things. He frowned because he was thinking really hard about something for a change.

Cycling along the lane away from the bungalow he had another surprise. A troop of children walked and jumped and pushed each other on the road ahead. As Justin came level with them he saw that it was the Ridett family. They were unusually clean and tidy. Justin jammed on his brakes and teetered beside Sandy.

"You'll wreck your tyres if you stop like that," Sandy told him. "Where are you going, anyway?"

Justin swerved and pretended not to hear. He wanted to keep his expedition to himself. "You lot look as if you're going for a picnic," he said, "only you haven't any bags for eats. Do you just walk to nowhere special?"

"We're going to Sunday school, of course," called

little Kate, who was trying to push Mark off the grass bank.

Justin was surprised that he nearly fell off his cycle altogether.

"What, all of you? I thought it was only a thing for little kids! And where d'you have to go, anyway?"

Carol, as usual, was the giver of information. "Sandy and I help teach the little ones. We take a batch of them and help them to paint and make things while Mr Williams talks to the nines and tens for a while. It isn't easy for one teacher to keep a lot of mixed ages interested. I tell the little ones a Bible story they can understand while they paint, but of course we all have hymns and prayers and readings together afterwards. If you're so curious, why don't you come? You must know the little church near Widdens Halt. This is the longest way round to it, but it's not so dull as the main road."

Hastily Justin said, "No thank you", and that he was in a hurry. He shot away down the lane followed by shouts and cat-calls.

"Come and dig again tomorrow night!" yelled Pete. "We need at least five barrows more stones to finish that job!"

Justin waved to show he had heard, but he didn't look back. He could imagine Carol enjoying bossing the little kids around, but not Sandy. Pete and Mark, he supposed, were among the nines and tens who did something with Mr Williams, and it seemed as though they really liked it!

"But they won't catch me!" said Justin aloud, as he pedalled fast round a bend. "School's bad enough without doing something else indoors on a Sunday."

Five minutes later he turned down a narrower lane

and came to a halt beside a stile. The field beyond it was so full of flints that he really wondered how it could be ploughed. It sloped away gently from a bank crowned by a hazel coppice. Primroses in there, thought Justin. I might pick some for Mum when I get tired of stone-hunting.

With that in mind he heaved his cycle up on the stile and down the other side. I suppose I'd better not leave it too near the lane, he thought, and carried it some way along the bank. The bells from Widdens Cross came faintly across the fields. The sound seemed to add to the peace and beauty of the morning.

They're ringing frightfully early, or else my watch is slow, thought Justin, and then forgot them as he began his search.

After twenty minutes of stooping along the edge of the field, turning massive flints out of the red-brown earth, Justin stood up and stretched. There were flints in every kind of weird shape, some tiny, some almost too big for him to lift, but there was not one puddy stone. Justin began to realise why they were such treasures to those who found them.

"I suppose I could go on for weeks and there might not be one in the whole whopping field," he grumbled to himself. Then, as he stood with his hands in his pockets looking along the ridge where the brown earth joined the turf, he noticed a patch of chalky mould where some animal had probably been digging.

Might be a badger! thought Justin with interest, and he scrambled along the hammocky grass to have a look. Certainly something much bigger than rabbits had dug that hole, but whatever it was hadn't gone down very far. Not very far, but far enough to uncover a long ridge of metal which looked quite out of place at the edge of the hazel banks.

Justin ran the trowel he carried along the hard edge of it, scraping away dirt to show steely grey underneath.

A piece of farm machinery? he wondered, but somehow he didn't think it was that. Farm implements didn't get buried under turf as a rule. With quickening excitement he dug away the grass and mould, laying bare more and more of the peculiar blade. It went downwards at a steep angle, which made him wish he had a spade instead of a trowel.

This would be a job for The Crossing Kids, he thought, knowing how they would all burrow at it till they unearthed the whole thing. Then he thought of Anne. She would be at her cottage with all the windows open, writing her Sunday letter to her father. There was sure to be a spade in her garden shed.

From where he stood he could see the red roofs of Stannard's Cross just two fields away. Not wanting to heave his cycle over the stile again Justin set off towards a field gate he could see, keeping along by the hedges, and startling a pair of partridges as he went. It would probably have been quicker to ride round by the road, but it was fun going across country, and exceedingly muddy as well.

Anne, sitting where the sun came in at the bay window of the tiny cottage, was startled when she saw him. Scribbling away on page after page of airmail paper to her beloved father, she didn't hear the click of the gate. Justin's tousled head appearing above the window-sill made her jump. "What on earth!" she exclaimed, not looking too pleased, but Justin swung himself up and sat on the sill.

"You're wanted!" he told her. "You and a jolly good spade. I've been looking for puddy stones in the flint field by the Widdens lane, and I've unearthed something pretty queer. Be a sport and do that letter presently. The thing I've found is too big for me to manage."

Anne grumbled a little as she went round shutting windows, and then she stopped to change out of the fresh yellow Sunday frock she was wearing. One look at Justin's muddy jeans had told her that it wasn't going to be a clean expedition. But once she was out in the sunshine, showing Justin a quicker way across the fields, she began to enjoy herself.

"Listen to those larks!" she said. "They sound as though they just have to sing hymns of praise for being able to fly right up into the blue—I don't believe that hymns were meant to be sung only inside a church, anyway!"

Justin, who was trotting ahead, half turned and looked at her in a puzzled way. "D'you often think about God?" he asked. "I never do, or almost never. Mum does, I suppose. She goes to church sometimes, but that sort of thing never seems real to me."

"But of course God is real!" Anne laughed as she said it, a laugh that had gaiety and certainty in it. "He's as real as you are. As real as this lovely wind that's blowing over our faces. We can't see it, but we can feel it. I'd be miserable, with Mother in hospital and Daddy so far away, if I didn't know that God is caring for us all every minute of the day."

"You're odd, you are," said Justin, because he didn't know quite how to reply, and ran ahead so that she had to chase him to keep up.

"My hat! It *is* queer!" exclaimed Anne a couple of

minutes later, as she bent over the long shaft of metal. "Here—give me that trowel. I'll scrape it clean as you shift the earth away. I think we're only seeing the tip of something really big. I wish Sandy was here; he might have an idea what it is."

They worked furiously, getting out of breath and having to slow down. Then they discovered that the piece of metal, although long, was not so very wide.

"Let's dig out the top of it, which must almost stick out of the bank above us," suggested Anne; "there are hazel roots going right over it, but I can work those loose."

Suddenly Justin gave a shout. "I know what it is!" he cried. "It's an aeroplane propeller! This is the curved tip of the blade!"

CHAPTER FOUR

A DROP IN THE DARK

Justin sat down on a hummock of turf above the blade and ran the edge of his spade along the length of it. "Then this is a bit of the old war," he said. "I wonder why someone hasn't taken it away."

Down below him, scrabbling with the trowel, Anne thought about it. "I guess no one knew," she said. "Grandma told me lots of planes were shot down in fights over Kent. If one broke up in the air the pieces sometimes fell miles apart. This edge of the field is above the plough line, and in a whole summer I guess weeds would have covered a thing that had half buried itself. It would have been hidden by harvest time."

"Let's dig around the middle bit. I suppose it's too much to hope that the other blade is whole." Justin set to work again, remembering the films he had seen about the Battle of Britain. It all seemed so long ago. Just a bit of history like all the things in Mr Cassidy's collection.

It was Anne who first felt the earth move under them. She was prising away the clinging turf from the place where they guessed the middle of the propeller must be, when she saw the blade move just a fraction of its own accord. "It's coming loose!" she cried with delight. "I believe that if we both heave on the part we can see we might shift the whole thing!"

"It's moving! It's tilting up!" shouted Justin, and they grabbed at the metal, sure that they could pull it away.

But as they did so something else began to happen, and it happened so quickly. The propeller blade tilted up and knocked Anne flying. Justin, trying to hold it, felt his feet sliding down as though hands were pulling them. He tried to shout to Anne to get clear, but there was a great rumbling sound as the propeller tore out of his hands and shot down into a great hole which was opening under them. Earth, flints, turf and rocks were all falling inwards, and with them went Justin.

Anne rolled over, and could perhaps have scrambled clear, but seeing her friend disappearing she made a wild grab at his anorak and found herself sliding too. The next moment she was half blinded by crumbling earth, and her long plaits fell across her face, and threatened to suffocate her.

It was some minutes before Anne was thinking clearly again. She came to herself, spitting out hair and chalk, and found that she had a terrific pain in her shoulder, and that her head was aching. After the bright sunshine in the field above, the place where she lay seemed very dim, but a patch of light above her outlined the hole through which they had fallen.

"Justin," she said, thickly, finding her mouth dry and speaking difficult. "Justin—where are you?"

For a moment there was no answer. Then an enormous sneeze came from the darkness beyond Anne's feet. "Coo! I thought I'd killed myself!" came Justin's voice following the sneeze. "Are you all right, Anne? Wherever are we?"

Shuffling noises and yelps of pain told that Justin

was getting up. "Don't kick me," said Anne, hastily, finding the words coming easily again now that she knew Justin was there.

As their eyes got used to the dimness they realised that they were quite a long drop from the surface, and that there was space around them. A lot of rubble had fallen as well, but beyond it there was standing stonework. The propeller which had begun all the trouble was there with them. It was tilted at an angle, with its tip towards the light, and part of the other blade, broken off in the middle, was underneath Justin.

"I believe we're in an old well shaft," he said, anxiously, when he had felt himself all over and decided that no bones were broken. "It's going to be an awful job to get out."

Anne tried to sit up, and found she could manage it. The worst of the headache was passing, though her shoulder was agony to touch.

"I don't think it's a well," she said shakily. "It's much too wide, and there's a stone arch behind you. I think we're in some sort of cellar."

"Well, the quicker we get out of it the better," said Justin. "I must have given myself an awful jolt by the feel of my knees, and I guess we'll both ache like billy-o tomorrow. But isn't it great finding a place like this? Just wait till we tell Sandy!"

Anne wasn't so sure that it was great. She knew that it must be getting on for dinner time, and that Aunt Madge would expect her to come cycling home very soon. Justin rather stiffly turned himself round to look at the stone arch which Anne said she could see. "There really is an arch!" he said. "I thought you were dreaming things because you banged your head!

There's a tiny little doorway, but it's nearly full of rocks and rubbish. There's a space beyond it, though —I can feel cold air."

"And I can smell it!" Painfully Anne got up and stood beside him. "D'you know what I think," she said. "I think this is part of somewhere very old; maybe it's been overgrown for centuries. Then that bit of plane came crashing down on top of it and broke through, but it got stuck."

"And we started digging and finished the job!" agreed Justin. "But the rabbits or a badger must have dug first."

"And hit the metal, so they couldn't go down any further!"

For a minute or two they forgot their own danger in the interest of piecing the story together. The three-foot gap at the top of the arch told them that there was a hollow space beyond. When they shouted, a dull echo came back.

It wasn't long, though, before hunger, as well as Justin's watch with its luminous hands, told them it was high time to escape. Then their spirits sank considerably. However much he tried, Justin couldn't get footholds or handholds on the sheer stonework of the wall beside them. On the other side a steep bank of earth and rubble and tree-roots rose to the broken roof. There, around the gaping hole, pieces of stonework showed against the sky, leaning at dangerous angles. They were only held in place by the weight of earth still partly holding them. They would probably come crashing down all too easily. There was nothing to climb up on, and they realised that they were trapped as neatly as mice in a milk bottle.

"Well, I'm not going to worry," said Anne; "two

people can't just vanish without a search party being around pretty soon. There's one thing we can do which is best of all. We can tell God about it."

Standing there in the dim light Anne folded her hands and bent her head. Justin stood awkwardly beside her, looking up at the patch of sky. If God is supposed to love us, and knows all about us, he thought, why didn't He stop us falling down this wretched hole? Aloud he said, "D'you really believe He'll hear your prayer, and do something about it?"

Anne didn't answer for a minute, and then she opened her eyes and said very certainly, "Of course I do! God knows we're here, and why. It seems just like an accident, and it may be just that, but perhaps there's a reason for it happening that we'll know one day. What did you do with that spade?" she added, changing the subject. "If it fell in with us it must be somewhere around. Maybe if we could push the earth away from that little arch we might find a way out."

They started to search, kicking at the newly fallen earth around them. At first it seemed as though the spade must have stayed above ground, caught by some root or rock. Then, just as they were giving up hope of finding anything, Anne caught her toe in something and nearly fell. "I've found it! I've got my toe in the handle!" she cried joyfully. "Help me to wriggle it free, and we can do something at last!"

It was a good thing they found the spade. Having something to do helped Justin to forget his rising fear of being trapped. He had never outgrown a fear he had had as a little boy of being in small, dark places, even during riotous games of 'Find the Robber'.

They took turns to work at the small, blocked doorway, and found the earth and rubbish that filled it surprisingly soft. In twenty minutes they had a sizeable hole. By that time their eyes had grown accustomed to the dimness, and when Justin lay on his stomach and wriggled forward through the arch he could see faint outlines ahead of him.

"There are pillars!" he cried. "Round ones—very thick. I believe it's a dungeon, or a church!"

"Let me see!" Anne pushed in beside him, and gave a cry of anguish as her shoulder bumped against the stonework.

"It's not as big as that," she said, "I still think it's a cellar. But there's light coming from somewhere over there. Not much, but it might be another hole."

Very cautiously Justin edged forward, making the earth crumble away in front of him. He could hear it plopping down on something below, and wished desperately that they had a torch or matches.

"I'll have to turn round," he said. "I'd rather not fall head first. You hang on to the hood of my anorak and help to let me down gently, or pull me up if I can't find anything to stand on."

It took some minutes to get him in the right position, and Anne had to bite her lips because holding hard to his anorak sent pain shooting up her arm.

"Easy does it," came Justin's muffled voice, and she could hear his feet scrabbling, and the falling of stones. Then he cried, "O.K.! I'm standing on something—you can let me go."

Five minutes later Anne was through the hole herself and standing beside him, feeling a faint waft of air blowing on her face. Cautiously, clinging together in case they fell, they moved forward. Sturdy pillars rose on either side of the strange place, and once they got beyond the rubble the floor was paved with great stone slabs. Then they saw the reason for the light. High above them in the arching roof there was a hole several inches across. A thick tree root came down through it and twined around the top of a pillar. The shaft of light which streamed down from the hole showed them that they were in a small chapel, or crypt, for on a great stone altar was marked the outline of a cross.

"It's a forgotten church we've found!" cried Anne, feeling both awe and excitement, and then she gave a cry of joy. On the altar slab were several round stones, and as she picked one up her fingers found the indented pattern on it. "They're puddy stones!" she exclaimed. "Five of them in this strange place!"

Justin took them one by one and felt the patterns. "The people who put them here thought of them as treasures," he said. "Queer, isn't it? I came to find a puddy stone and we've found five!" Then he added, soberly, "But stones won't do us a lot of good if we can't get out."

Anne traced the cross again with her fingers, and said, quietly, "I'm sure we'll get out. Not today, perhaps, or even tomorrow. I'm just sorry for all the bother we'll be causing. I know this much," she added, thoughtfully; "when they realise we're missing they'll be praying for us as well as working to find us. Most of all young Kate will. She's got terrific faith, you know."

"But she's only seven!" cried Justin. "What good would her prayers do?"

"All the good in the world, I'd say," Anne told him. "She thanks God for all sorts of things, and she asks for help, or to be forgiven just like she'd ask her daddy. Carol tells me about it, and says she's the kindest little soul. I'm quite a lot comforted to know that little Kate will be praying when she knows something's happened to us."

"You are odd!" Justin told her for the second time, but he turned the puddy stone in his hand and his fingers found the pattern strangely comforting. Long, long ago someone had treasured it because it carried the sign of the cross. Their faith, like small Kate's, must have been very simple and trustful. Perhaps those far-off people, and the little girl with freckles on her nose, shared some great secret. Suddenly Justin wished he could share it, too.

CHAPTER FIVE

SEARCH PARTY

It was a good thing that Justin had decided to go looking for puddy stones in the morning. Two children not returning in time for their tea on a very fine day would not have caused a lot of worry. Both had friends who might invite them, and both were trusted to come home in plenty of time for supper. But missing their Sunday dinner was another thing.

Aunt Madge waited half an hour, getting more and more annoyed, and old Mr and Mrs Lott, who fed Justin on his mother's 'hospital Sundays' were both cross and anxious as the clock ticked on past two.

"That young man will get the edge of my tongue when he shows up," grumbled Mr Lott, cutting his overcooked meat and eating it without pleasure.

"That he will! I made him a jam roly because he asked for it specially!" complained the old lady.

Aunt Madge rang the Ridetts, sure that Anne had looked in there on her way back from the cottage. She was puzzled, because Anne was such a good girl for time-keeping. "We haven't seen her!" exclaimed Mrs Ridett. "I know she told Carol last night that she'd be going to church in the evening."

The Ridetts settled back to finish their Sunday meal, sure that there was some simple explanation. Then Pete had an idea. "I wonder if she's doing something with Justin," he said, rather thickly, through a slice of apple-pie. "We saw him this morning when we were going to Sunday school. He was heading towards Mr Cassidy's, I think."

"He was in a hurry," said Kate. "He didn't want to talk to us a bit."

Half an hour later Mr Lott came through the level-crossing and knocked on their door. "Is young Justin with you?" he asked. "We've not seen hair nor hide of him today, except when he looked in for a minute after breakfast. His mother left at half past eight, of course; but he slept on till nine, so he said. He dropped a hint that he'd like a jam roly for his dinner, too, which was taking a liberty. but the wife made it and he's not been in to eat it. I've been asking round all the houses where he knows the children. I want to know just what he's been up to before his mother comes back."

That made Mrs Ridett really worried. Carol and Sandy came and stood close to her while she tried to think what Mr Lott could do next. "Daddy is over at Flaxenham for their special Anniversary Services today," she said, "or he'd take you over to Mr Cassidy's in the car. There's just a chance that both children might be there doing something with those treasures of his."

"But Anne wouldn't overstay and worry her aunt; she's too sensible," said Carol, quickly. "I believe they've had an accident."

"Well, I suppose I could ring up Mr Cassidy," said Mr Lott, doubtfully, only to be told that the old gentleman refused to have a telephone.

In the end The Level-crossing Kids organised a search party. While the bigger boys hared off to Mr Cassidy's on their cycles, Carol took Kate and Mark to see Anne's Aunt Madge. "And then we'll hunt along the small lanes towards Widdens," said Carol. "After all, they may not be together, and Anne might just have come home that way for a change and fallen off for some silly reason, and hurt herself." She turned to call Kate to hurry up, but Kate was standing with her hands folded just as though she were in church. Bless her! She's telling God about it! thought Carol, who had done the same thing half an hour before.

When they all reached home again no one was any the wiser, but all of them were a lot more bothered. There seemed nothing for it but to inform the police, though Aunt Madge felt they should wait till Justin's mother came off duty.

"She'll be home in half an hour," she said. "Those nursing auxiliaries, or whatever they call them, come home early on Sundays. She may even have an idea where Justin might be. He might only have forgotten to tell Mrs Lott."

"But there was the roly pudding," said Kate.

The children moped about, feeling restless and unhappy, and it was then that Kate remembered the primroses. "We promised to pick them!" she cried. "A whole lot of bunches for teacher to post to those invalid children. You know we promised, Mark, and we've both forgotten!"

"Well, you'll have to hurry," her mother told her, feeling that it might be a good thing for the younger ones to have something to do while they were worrying about their friends. "Don't be late for tea, whatever you do. I'm playing the organ tonight, remember."

There was a scurry for baskets, and then an argument as to where picking would be easiest. "There's most at the edge of the flinty field," said Mark. "That one sloping away from Widdens Lane. It won't take us long if we run all the way, and there's so many that we'll get them in no time."

"It's much too far!" Pete told him definitely, and then the tooting of a car horn made them look up. "Want a lift anywhere, you three?" asked their friend the Vet, cheerfully. "You're all looking as solemn as owls."

"Oh! yes please! As far as the primrose bank near to your house," cried Pete. "We've got to pick a lot in a hurry, and if you take us there we can run all the way home in time for tea."

"I'll just tell Mum who's taking us," said Mark, sensibly, and Kate was already climbing in beside Mr Marley. "We've got to be quick because Mummy's playing the organ tonight," she explained, as she settled in the passenger seat. "I'm going to church as well because Justin and Anne have got lost and I guess we'll be asking God to help them."

Mr Marley was interested, and anxious, too, when Pete explained. "I'd go straight to the police if I were you," he said. "Anyway, I'll keep a watch out this afternoon. I have to go over to Beresford Farm, and I might see or hear something."

He set them down near the stile, and waved goodbye as they scrambled over. "That's saved us half an hour," said Pete, with satisfaction, and Kate was already running ahead along the grass ridge at the edge of the ploughed earth. A moment later she stopped and said in a disappointed voice, "There's people picking already. There's someone's bike left on the bank."

"Plenty for everyone, I guess," Mark told her, seeing the mist of yellow between the hazel bushes. And then, as he stopped a moment to glance at the bright blue cycle lying on its side, he gave a shout. "It's Justin's bike! I'm sure it is!"

Pete caught them up and said, quickly, "If it's got his initials scratched under the saddle, that's certain. I heard him telling Sandy that was the best way to prove who it belonged to if it got stolen. Help me heave it over, Mark."

"It is! It is! It's Justin's!" they cried, when they could see the underside of the saddle. There, quite clearly marked, were the letters 'J.T.W.'.

"But what's he doing here?" exclaimed Pete. "I can't imagine Justin coming after primroses."

Kate turned away from the bicycle and looked across the field with its countless flints showing in the brown soil. "He might be looking for special stones," she said.

"Well, if he was doing that we'd see him!" Mark told her, loftily.

It was Pete, as the elder, who decided what they should do.

"I could ride this bike if I sit on the bar," he said. "I vote I ride it home and tell them we've found it. You can scout around the wood looking for clues, Mark, and Katie can pick her primroses double quick. Don't go further than a shout from the stile, either of you. I guess Sandy or Carol will ride back and fetch you, and see if you've found anything."

Mark helped him to heave the cycle over the stile and he went wobbling off on it, uncomfortable because his legs were shorter than Justin's. Kate was already picking primroses all round her, and tying little bunches with strands of wool. It was very quiet.

There was no sound of anyone else in the wood behind her, only a lark soaring higher and higher over the field, singing as it went.

Mark came back to her and picked a few flowers just to keep her company. "Now I'm going to tramp around the wood a bit," he said. "Old Justin could be stuck up a tree and scared to get down, I suppose."

Kate went on picking, hearing the snap of rotten branches as Mark scuffed his way into the wood. Every now and then he called, "Coo-ee!" but there was no answer.

Then Kate, sitting on the primrose bank tying her bunches, lifted her head and listened. Very faintly she heard another sound, and felt her skin prickle with the strangeness of it. "People singing," she said to herself in a whisper. "People in the field singing—but there's no one there!" For a moment she crouched like a small rabbit, frightened to move, and then she heard Mark coming back.

"There's not a thing..." he began, and then saw that Kate had her finger to her lips for silence, and her eyes were very wide.

"What is it?" he whispered, and then he heard it, too.

"People singing. But they sound smothered, somehow." For a moment they both listened, and then the sound stopped. "I know what that was," said Mark. "It was someone's radio and they've turned it off. There may be a car in the layby down the road, and the sound came across the field. I hope old Sandy hurries up and comes to fetch us."

"Well, do a bit of picking, then," said little Kate, disappointed because the magical sound of the singing was something so ordinary. She got up and wandered along the grass bank a little way, to where the sun was warmer. Then, looking ahead to where the field and the wood curved round together, she exclaimed, "Oh! Mark—look! There's the biggest rabbit hole I've ever seen, over there! Can we go and see it?"

Mark preferred anything to picking primroses, and together they ran to the great gash they could see in the greenness where the trees ended. They had almost reached it when Mark stopped so suddenly that his sister nearly fell over him. From under their feet, it seemed, the sound of singing came again:

"The Lord's my shepherd; I'll not want." Words they knew so very well, but here they had an eerie sound. Mark clutched Kate and felt his heart pounding. The big hole looked strange enough, but the voices were a lot stranger. Between excitement and fear Mark found his own voice. "Who's there?" he called. "Are you real, or aren't you?"

There was no doubt about the answer. "Help! He-l-p!" came two voices in unison. "It's Anne and Justin! We're trapped!"

With a squeal of joy Kate dashed forward, only to be stopped by another shout. "Come carefully—the ground's all breaking!"

Actually it was several minutes before they could look down into the hole. As soon as they got close to it from any direction, the earth began to crumble in a frightening manner. A yelp from Anne told them that they were sending stones bouncing down. Then Mark, scouting carefully round by the hazel bushes, found a place where it seemed firm. He lay down flat and wriggled forward. A good many feet below he could see the top of Justin's head. Anne was further in the shadows.

"Hey!" he shouted. "Here we are! How long have you been down there?" Justin looked up with a grin of relief. "We fell in about twelve, I guess, but it feels like days ago. The ground just opened under us. Have you got anything to eat? We're starving!"

Mark had a couple of very squashed toffees in his pocket and he threw them down. "Everyone's in a state because you're lost," he said. "I'll go just as fast as I can and tell someone you're here."

He wriggled backwards from the hole, and Anne called up quite cheerfully, "You might ask them to bring along a Swiss roll or something, or I'll be too weak to be rescued!"

'I'll tell Kate..." began Mark, but when he got to his feet little Kate had vanished.

"Now where's she got to!" Mark stood a moment, feeling cross instead of racing off for help. He was responsible for Kate, and terrified that she might have fallen down some other hole. And then he saw her. Right away by the stile she was running and waving her basket, and shouting to someone who was coming along the lane.

A moment later Mark saw with relief that it was Mr Cassidy.

CHAPTER SIX

A LADDER INTO SUNSHINE

Mr Cassidy came tramping along the grass bank at tremendous speed, with Kate chattering beside him. He made his way with caution to the only safe place, which Mark had found.

"Undoubtedly this subsidence could have uncovered something most important," he said, with a good deal of excitement in his voice. "Of course, care must be taken not to damage anything which may be down below. Now, I wonder what is the best way to get down without causing a further landslide. It may be just a natural cavity we have here, or it could be a stone-age granary which has collapsed."

He got down on his knees stiffly, peered into the hole and saw Justin. Anne was sitting on a heap of rubble, thankfully sucking a toffee.

"Ah, my boy!" exclaimed Mr Cassidy. "You seem to have discovered an underground cavern. Most interesting, most interesting. I shall have to get down somewhat more carefully than you did, but I am most anxious to see the extent of this depression."

"But we're worrying about us getting up, not anybody getting down!" cried Justin. "It may be awfully exciting, but we want to get out!"

"There's a room at the back of this, Mr Cassidy!" called Anne, swallowing the last of her toffee. "It's got tree roots coming through the roof, and I think it's awfully old."

"A room? Really a room?" Mr Cassidy sounded so excited that Justin was afraid he might overbalance and tumble down on top of them, but just at that moment shouts from the field made him look round. Running along the grass bank came Sandy and Carol, with Pete panting behind them. They had caught a glimpse of Mark's bright blue anorak by the hazels.

Then things began to happen quickly. After the first relief and delight that the search was over, practical Carol decided at once what she must do. "I ought to go back right away and tell Justin's mother and Anne's that you're both all right," she said. "I'll bring some cake and stuff, and throw it down if you're not up by that time."

Anne called up, "Are they frightfully worried?"

"Worried stiff, of course," Carol told her. "But they won't have to bother the police now. When Pete arrived on your bike, Justin, they decided to wait a little longer."

"But the police must know!" Mr Cassidy scrambled up and dusted his knees. "They must be told, and so must the farmer who owns the field. This hole is a danger to the public now. Don't ride home, child. Go to Mr Marley's house byond the trees; he has a phone."

"We know—he's our vet. Why didn't we think!" Sandy was gone before he could get any more instructions, and Carol followed him, sure that Mrs Marley could find some food for the starving prisoners.

"What we need," said Mr Cassidy, suddenly, "is a ladder. Run, Mark; catch your sister. Tell her to ask if we may borrow Mr Marley's—I think he has an extending one."

In all the excitement they had forgotten Kate, but Kate hadn't forgotten her promise. Just behind them in the hazel coppice she was still picking primroses, and a basket and a half were filled with little bunches. She felt as excited as the others that Justin and Anne were found, and as she worked she said softly, "Thank You. Thank You for hearing our prayers and sending us here. And please," she added, "don't let them slip as they climb up."

It was quite a little while before they did climb up, because a ladder is an awkward thing to carry, and to get over a stile. While they waited the prisoners called up to Mr Cassidy, and no one was more surprised than he when they described the propeller which had started it all. "From the World War, undoubtedly," he said. "Pieces of planes fell all over the place in those days. I'm afraid you both had a very frightening experience."

"I was scared stiff," Justin admitted. "It was Anne who was brave. She was sure we'd be found."

"Only because I knew that God takes care of us," said Anne, quickly. "I can't say I liked it, all the same. Finding the room-place was exciting, though. I'm just longing for you to see it, Mr Cassidy, because I think it's a chapel. It feels a whole lot more exciting now we know we're safe."

"Ah!" said the old man, quietly, "I think you have discovered something that's better than the propeller or the cavern. You have learned to put your trust in God, and that makes it a great day."

Justin stopped looking up at the bright patch of sky, and kicked the rubble at his feet. He had sung the folk songs and the hymns with Anne just to keep her company, but when he had repeated a prayer after her he had seemed to be speaking into emptiness. Why couldn't he be like the others? he wondered. It seemed as though they felt God close beside them, and they were so sure.

At last voices told them that the ladder had arrived. "Stand right back," called Sandy; "we might send one or two clods down however careful we are, and we don't want to brain you!"

Hastily they pressed back against the stonework and watched as inch by inch the ladder came down towards them. Some earth and stones did fall but missed Justin's feet by inches. "Ladies first!" called Sandy, and Anne suddenly found that her knees felt very weak now that safety was so near. Justin could hardly wait for her to disappear into daylight before he began to climb. Hands reached out to him, and he found Pete and Sandy lying by the edge of the hole.

"Easy does it!" cautioned Sandy.

The sunlight seemed blinding as Justin crawled forward and then stood up. The hazel copse, the golden evening sky, and Anne sitting on the grass eating a huge hunk of cake all looked too bright to be real. It was then that Justin found that he simply must thank someone for being alive. Not just his friends who had come to the rescue, but someone unseen who had kept them safe, and alive, to climb into that clear air again. Aloud, he said, "Oh! boy! Does this feel good!" But in his heart, for the very first time, he said, "Thank You, God!" And he meant it.

The policeman and the farmer arrived together a few moments later, and promised to retrieve the spade and the ladder before dark. Kindly Mrs Marley had telephoned them both. When the children arrived at the house in the lane she took charge of Anne and Justin and skilfully attended to some very painful scratches and bruises which they both had to show for their day's adventure. Anne's tender shoulder she could do nothing about. "Just a nasty wrench, I'd think," she said. "I should let the doctor see it tomorrow." Thankfully they accepted tea, and the vet himself returned in time to offer them a lift home. Mark and Pete piled into the back seat with Justin, and Kate squashed in between them with her baskets.

"I expect Mr Cassidy is as pleased as a dog with two tails," said Mr Marley, as Anne slid thankfully into the passenger seat. "Underground caverns are just his line, but I doubt the farmer is very happy; he'll probably want the hole filled in."

"Oh! no!" cried Justin. "That old place wants exploring properly. If we have a ladder ready to get out with, I want to go down with a torch. Why, there might be buried treasure!"

"And there's our propeller, too!" protested Anne. "That's a trophy to remember the day by. As if we'd ever forget!"

As they drove round a bend in the lane the sound of bells came to them across the fields. "That's evening service at Widdens," said Pete. "Mum won't be at home; she's playing the organ at our church tonight. She told Sandy that she'd expect some of us there if we got back in time to get clean. We phoned her from your house, Mr Marley."

"You don't look too grubby to me," said Mr Marley. "I'll drop you three at church, if you like. I expect Sandy and Carol will just about get there on their cycles. You'll be saying a big 'thank you' because this day's adventure wasn't a tragedy."

Anne said, "Aunt Madge would be there, too, if it

wasn't for me messing things up. I'd have liked to slip in at the back, just because it's so wonderful to be alive. I guess Auntie's wanting me back, though."

"Well, she'd understand, I'm sure. I'll look in at your place and make it right with her as I go by," Mr Marley offered.

To his own surprise Justin found himself saying, "Could you do the same for my mum, please? I guess she won't mind if I don't get back for another hour, and even if we two are fearfully grubby we can explain afterwards."

It was a pity that Monday morning meant school. Both Justin and Anne woke with sundry big bruises still very tender, and they ached in all sorts of places, but both were longing to see what was happening to their hole. Justin's mother promised to ring up Anne's Aunt Madge before she went on duty at mid-day to say that he would come and see Anne after school. "But no getting down that hole again without plenty of people to help," she warned. "And you must have the farmer's approval, you know. He could have said that you were trespassing yesterday."

That idea alarmed Justin a bit, but he simply had to find out about the hole. That morning, in spite of the aches and pains, he was feeling tremendously happy. Since that moment when he had come up into the sunshine, and felt the need to say 'thank you', it was as though he had pushed a door open just a little way. As though he had glimpsed a golden light on the other side and knew that some glorious adventure lay ahead. It was a feeling he had no words to describe.

The bus seemed to crawl home from school that day, and there was no sign of anyone around the house by the level-crossing.

Guess they've got tired of their stone quarry, thought Justin, and he wondered if Carol and Sandy would want to explore the hole as well. His own homework, he had decided, would have to be done in the morning. He had promised his mother faithfully that he would get up an hour early if she would set the alarm.

His tea was scrambled through, and when he wheeled his cycle from the shed he was still munching a piece of jam tart. Riding towards the cottage at speed, he wondered what Anne was doing about homework. He guessed she was the sort of person who would do her best with it however early she had to get up in the morning.

Anne opened the door even before he had leaned his cycle against the wall. "Mr Cassidy left a message," she said, jubilantly. "It's simply splendid! He's going to be at the hole by five, and we're to get there as soon as we can. He'll have lights and a ladder, he says, and Mr Priddy, the antiquarian, will be there, too."

"Come in!" called Anne's Aunt Madge, hospitably, from an open window, but Anne and Justin were much too anxious to be on their way.

They could see quite a group of men standing by the hazel copse as they heaved their bicycles over the stile a little later. Mr Bryce, the farmer, had brought his teenage son along, and they had put planks round the edge of the hole to make it safer.

"So you're the discoverers, are you?" grinned Mr Bryce, as Anne and Justin arrived, a good deal out of breath. "My lad and I have brought up that propeller you found. Reckon you'll want the bits for keepsakes, if they're not claimed for any reason."

There it lay in the sunshine, the treasure they had found, scraped clean, and so much bigger than the puddy stone Justin had searched for.

"I think I had better go down first," said Mr Priddy, when the children had been introduced. "I'll make a nice cushion if by chance Mr Cassidy should slip! I imagine it's a while since you scrambled up and down a ladder, sir!"

"Longer than you might think," grunted Mr Cassidy, getting stiffly down on his knees. "But I wouldn't miss taking a look down this 'rabbit hole' for all the tea in China!"

The space at the bottom seemed very small when they were all standing down there, but during the morning Mr Bryce and his boy had carefully dug away more of the earth blocking the little archway, so that Mr Cassidy could edge his bulky form through without too much difficulty.

Justin watched the beam of the torch go sweeping round the walls of the hidden place which had been forgotten for so long. Only a few hours ago he had been trapped there with a feeling of fear like lead on his heart. Now it was quite, quite different. Not only because people were with him, and a ladder back to freedom stood a few feet away. It was different because he knew for certain that there was another presence there. Someone who had known all about the ancient people who had built that place, and their hopes and fears so long ago.

I guess I'll never feel quite alone again, not as long as I live, thought Justin. I guess I've found out what little Kate feels like when she talks to God. He's close beside us all the time—for ever and ever.

CHAPTER SEVEN

THE GOLDEN BAND

"This was undoubtedly a chapel," said Mr Cassidy, sending his torch light up to the curve of the roof, and over every inch of the stone slab on which the puddy stones lay. "See," he said, with excitement in his gruff old voice, "there's a blocked-up doorway on the south side. It has a flat top, and red Roman bricks edging it. The one we came in at is round-topped, and that will be much later. I believe people prayed in this place long before William the Conqueror."

"I would think it dates back to Augustine, at least," agreed Mr Priddy. He was kneeling below the place where the tree roots were coming through the roof, and was scooping away at the fallen mould and stones with a little trowel he carried.

Anne crouched beside him holding a torch, and watching as his fingers probed and searched the earth for small traces of the long-ago people. "Do you mean that they would have built this after Augustine came to Kent to teach people about God?" she asked, and Justin said, quickly, "But aren't the Roman walls older than that?"

For a minute or two they stopped exploring while Mr Cassidy explained that a tiny Roman temple could have stood there in ages past, and then when the Romans went away it fell into ruin. But a good princess called Bertha had come from France, and she had married the Kentish king. Bertha was a Christian, and that was some time in the year five hundred and sixty two, he said.

"She made a tiny little chapel outside the walls of Canterbury," Mr Priddy added, from the floor. "You can see it still. She used a Roman ruin for that, too, and now it's part of old St Martin's church. Perhaps Bertha and her king changed other little pagan temples into churches, as well. You see, she helped King Ethelbert to become a Christian, too."

Justin didn't mean to interrupt, but as Mr Cassidy's torch wavered he suddenly saw something that made him cry out in surprise.

"There's lettering all round the edge of that stone! I'm sure it's lettering, not just a pattern!" he exclaimed.

Mr Priddy scrambled up and came over to see. The great stone slab on top of the ancient altar certainly had deep marks cut in the edge of it, though many of them were nearly worn away by time. Mr Cassidy ran his hand over the marks as though he could see them with his finger tips. "Latin," he grunted. "Probably done a century or two later, but still early enough."

"What does it say?" Justin tried to pick out single letters for himself but he found it very hard. Some words were gone completely and others had only half their letters left, and Mr Cassidy tried for five minutes before he could get the sense of it. At last he said, "Earth—that's 'earth', for certain. And there's 'fulness' nearly at the end."

" 'The earth is the Lord's, and the fulness thereof'," quoted Mr Priddy. "I think, you know, that verse explains the presence of these fossil stones."

"You mean that people who found them in the

flinty fields thought they belonged to God because all the earth is His, and the puddy stones had a cross on them, and that made people think of Jesus?" Anne's words tumbled over each other in her excitement, and she wished that Kate had been with them just then.

Justin was imagining a long-ago shepherd, dressed in rough skins, leaving his sheep on the hillside and creeping in to put the puddy stones in the place where he felt they belonged. Then he remembered the tiny Roman coin Mr Cassidy had given him and thought that Bertha might have found some in the little pagan temple when she first came there. Perhaps she was quite as excited as we are when we find Roman coins, he thought; the Romans had been gone quite a time before she sailed over from France.

The two elderly men searched about, tapping walls for any sign of hollowness, and finding in a corner broken shards of pots which had perhaps held offerings of grain. Suddenly the voice of Mr Bryce came echoing down to them. "Time you were getting up!" he called. "Rain's coming on, and you'll get a fair soaking on the way home if you don't look slippy!"

"Dear, dear, I suppose we must go,' said Mr Cassidy, reluctantly. "I suppose the poor man is getting tired of waiting to steady the ladder and help us out."

"I still want to go on looking!" said Anne, rebelliously, putting Mr Priddy's torch down on the floor for a moment while she took a stone out of her shoe.

"I guess they'll let us come down again," murmured Justin, as the two men edged their way through the tiny arch. "Mr Priddy says he's bringing proper trained diggers to take bits of the paving up and see what's under the floor. I guess they'll let us look as well because we found the place."

He turned to follow where the beam of Mr Cassidy's torch was flickering beyond the arch, but suddenly Anne grabbed his elbow. "Wait!" she said, urgently. "I've seen something! Just as I picked this torch up—a tiny bit of yellow!"

She dropped on her knees close to the place where Mr Priddy had been searching and took hold of a piece of metal which showed above a scatter of loose earth. The rains of many winters had washed quite a pile of soil and dead leaves through the hole where the tree roots showed, but it was not a yellowed leaf that Anne saw.

She pulled gently, fearful of breaking anything, and part of a thin band of metal came into the torch light. Most of it was crusted with dirt, and it had little heart-shaped pendants hanging from it. One of them, surprisingly clean, showed truly golden, and had a pattern still clearly showing.

"Oh! be careful!" Justin warned. "If that's a treasure and you spoil it they'll be mad at you. There's Mr Bryce shouting again."

"I must get it," said Anne, stubbornly. "We fell into the hole, they didn't, so I don't see why they should have all the fun. Hold the torch for me—I need both hands."

She scrabbled with her fingers, pulling gently, and a second later the whole thing came free.

"You children down there! Come up at once!' came Mr Cassidy's commanding voice, and Justin obeyed with all speed. Anne following him towards the light, feeling all prickly with excitement.

"I'm coming, but I can't hurry," she called, and stopped a moment to tie her headband round the middle of her treasure. Taking the ribbon ends in her teeth she began to climb. She had been afraid to crush the frail thing into her pocket, and she needed both hands for the ladder.

Up at the top the grown-ups were impatient. The evening had turned dull and cold, and rain began to fall in earnest as Anne appeared. "Whatever——" began Mr Cassidy, as Justin helped her out, and then he saw the dangling object.

"A torque! A torque! Absolutely whole! Where did you see it, you amazing child?"

The rain was forgotten as they stood there passing the treasure from hand to hand. Wherever the encrusting dirt had fallen away the gold showed clearly, chased with that delicate patern, as lovely as the day when some ancient craftsman fashioned it.

"What's a torque? What's it for?" Justin wanted to know.

"An armband, or a necklet for a great lady," Mr Cassidy told him, and Justin felt that it was right that Anne should have found it.

"This is a most wonderful find. It's almost too much to hope that there may be others as fine." Mr Priddy stood gently burnishing a small section with his thumb. "Pure gold never tarnishes, you know, even if it's been in the earth, as this probably has, for around seventeen hundred years. I'm afraid I must be the one to take care of this for a while," he said to Anne. "You'll realise that a treasure like this must belong to the country, not to any one person, even though you had the honour of finding it."

"I own the ground," said Mr Bryce, quickly, "but I suppose I can't claim it, either?"

"There are a lot of legalities, I'm afraid," said Mr

Priddy, cheerfully. "I've no doubt, though that you will benefit in some way, in the end."

"And there's the propeller we found," put in Justin. "I'd like to have that more than anything."

"I don't think that's counted as treasure trove, but some Government department will probably want to see it before you have it to decorate your bedroom with," Mr Priddy told him with a chuckle.

The ladder was hauled up, and they went their various ways, Mr Priddy promising the children faithfully that they should know of everything that happened to their hole in the weeks to come.

As they rode home through the lanes, slowly in spite of the rain, Anne and Justin let their imaginations run riot. How did the golden band come to be there? Had it belonged to the French princess? Or to some great Saxon lady whose husband claimed the land from Widdens to the sea? It was a Roman ornament, Mr Priddy had said, but they could still have owned it, and counted it a great and ancient treasure.

"I'm going to get books about those old Romans, out of the reference library," said Justin, with enthusiasm. "If they made gorgeous things like that, they must have been jolly clever."

"And loved beauty," said Anne. Then she added, thoughtfully, "I think the French princess must have been jolly brave. If the Kentish king was a tough old pagan, I guess he had pagan warriors round him. Pagan priests, too! They may have been pretty horrible to her because she was a Christian. Probably some of them would have liked to kill her for it."

Justin rode smack through a wide puddle in the lane. "But she must have shown that being a Christian was a good thing," he called back, "or the king would never have changed to be one, too. I guess she was awfully patient. She must have been what my mum calls 'a stayer' and not let them get her down."

"I guess it's always been that way, right from the very beginning," Anne said, pedalling fast to catch up with him. "It can be pretty hard trying to be a Christian at school, or at home even, if things don't go the way you want, or someone gets nasty. Do you find it hard at your school? Do they tease the people who go to church? Quite a lot of our girls go, but some say it's only because their mothers make them."

"I don't find it hard because I don't go myself," Justin told her, honestly. "I came last night because I suddenly wanted to say 'thank you' to somebody for being alive. That's about all there is to it, though. I've just never thought about it before. God never seemed real till we got up out of that hole. Now I do believe He's there, and it's a nice feeling, but I don't very much want to be what you call 'a Christian'. Not if it means keeping a whole lot of rules or something like that."

Anne didn't answer for a moment or two. In her heart she was saying, "Please, God, help me to say the right thing. I do want Justin to be certain that Jesus wants him for a follower, and that He came to show us all what You are really like."

Actually she never had a chance to reply. There was a sudden shout from Justin, who braked hard, skidded on the wet road, and landed in a heap on the grass bank.

Head down against the rain, Sandy had come swishing round the corner. There was a sharp bend in the lane and he had taken that corner much too wide. The yell he gave warned Carol. She was following him, but at a sensible speed.

By the time she caught up, Anne was trying to help the boys out of a tangle of arms and legs and bicycle wheels.

CHAPTER EIGHT

BED AND BOREDOM

Afterwards, Justin couldn't remember a lot about what happened on that wet road. There was a terrible pain in his back when Anne tried to pull him free from the bicycle, and his head felt as though a mountain had hit it where his ear had met Sandy's handlebar.

Sandy had scrambled up more or less unhurt—which was a wonder, considering that he came down on top of pedals and spinning wheels. But Justin begged them to let him lie still, and that sent Carol racing to phone for an ambulance.

The next thing Justin remembered was his mother, in her nurse's uniform, bending over him. "Well! I didn't expect you to come and join me at the hospital!" she said, with an attempt at gaiety as his eyes opened; but even in his muzzy state Justin could tell that she was very concerned.

They all had a lot to be thankful for, because the accident could have been so much worse, but to his dismay Justin found that he would have to lie still for a fortnight or more, and then get back to his normal, energetic life very gradually.

"A nasty blow in the base of the spine," the doctor said. "That head of yours will feel like a turnip, as well, for a day or two, I'm afraid. This should teach you not to go larking about on a wet road."

Justin opened his mouth to say, "I wasn't larking! Sandy ran into me." But he changed his mind and said, lamely, "At least, I fell on the grass." One didn't tell tales on one's friends, but, all the same, he was sore at Sandy. Why couldn't the silly chump look where he was going!

Sandy, in fact, had ground away at his homework that day, had finished it early and persuaded Carol away from hers so that they could ride over and see if there was anything going on at the fabulous hole. After the crash he had been much too sobered to go and look.

Justin lay in bed and fumed. No football till next season, the doctor had told him, and that made his feeling against Sandy twice as bad. If Justin was in his element anywhere, it was on the football field. Almost his first visitor was the sports master from his school, anxious to know when their best centre forward would be fit again.

Then Mrs Ridett came to visit him, bringing Carol and Pete, and some books in case he could read lying on his back, and she said they had a lot to be thankful to God for, that the accident had been no worse.

"God isn't fair," muttered Justin, and refused to try to be cheerful. Nobody commented on that, but Carol put a big bunch of primroses and a few blue-bells on his bedside table. "Young Kate picked these for you," she said. "You should have heard her scolding Sandy for running into you!"

In spite of himself Justin grinned; but, after they had gone, the primroses reminded him of the hazel coppice, and the hole. He fumed all the more because something was bound to be happening there, and he would be out of it.

Everyone had told him that the consequences of the accident might have been far, far worse, but Justin absolutely refused to thank God for that. "If He's got anything to do with it, He's jolly mean to let the accident happen at all," he grumbled. Then he caught himself thinking with surprise, But I still know He's real! A while ago I would have thought, There isn't any God, so I don't have to be thankful, anyway. Now I know He's there, absolutely for certain, but I just think He's being mean.

It was Anne's visit that he looked forward to most, and when she came she brought exciting news. A team of diggers from a Kent society had been down to the ancient chapel, and under the floor they had found signs of a much earlier people than Queen Bertha and King Ethelbert. They had found a strange, old ring, and a part of a shield.

"They guess that whoever made the little chapel deliberately buried signs of the past, and put a new floor down, and began again," Anne told him. "A kind of way of saying that they were beginning a new life, looking to Jesus as their leader. I expect the pagan people round may have made things jolly hot for them even while they were building."

"I can't think why God shouldn't have made things go easily for them once they'd decided to believe in Him," muttered Justin, sourly, reaching for the glass of lemonade on his side table, and wincing at the pain in his back.

Anne cupped her chin in her hand and looked at him with a look that was more exasperation than pity. "Don't you see, you chump," she said, "that if God gave everyone free will, He can't keep on interfering. Because He's given them freedom, He can't stop them every time they're stupid, or jealous, or angry, or when they make wars and hurt other people. He helps the ones who want to serve Him to be brave, and happy, and make the best of things, and that helps us to grow into something worth while. If He made it easy all the time, we'd just be a lot of robots. We wouldn't be real people—just awfully wishy-washy, I guess."

Justin thought about that for a moment, and then he gave a big sigh and said, thoughtfully, "I suppose it would be like living in a world without any mountains. Nothing to climb."

Anne nodded. "Or playing football against a team that let you always win," she added, unaware that the very thought of football made Justin feel hard done by. They talked of other things, and Anne pulled out from the pocket of her jeans a tiny Chinese puzzle which he could work at for hours while lying flat.

"There you are," she said. "Mr Cassidy sent it. He says you can bring it back when you're getting round again. I saw Sandy yesterday," she added, as she got up to go. "He's feeling so bad about having run you down that he doesn't dare come to see you. He really is sorry."

She had expected a sulky look, but Justin surprised himself as well as Anne by saying, quickly, "Tell him not to be stupid. Of course he can come. Tell him I'll give him the thump he deserves, when I'm well!"

"And I'll probably get a rude answer!" said Anne, cheerfully, and she went on her way.

Lying there waiting for it to be supper time, Justin did a lot of thinking. The Chinese puzzle lay untouched on the coverlet while he pondered over some of the things that Anne had said. The result was that he considerably surprised his mother when she came in to sit with him as she came off duty.

"You'll be going to stay with Mr and Mrs Lott in a couple of days," she told him. "This bed is needed for another patient. You don't need any nursing, really, just rest now. The Lotts say you can be in your little room over there, and they'll see you don't starve. You know I'll be in to see you some time every day. Soon I shall have a long weekend off, and you can come home and be up most of the day. I'm afraid you'll be a bit bored, but the Lotts are very kind, and you can have your little radio."

"I'll be all right, don't you worry. I won't grouse or be a bother," said Justin. "I might even try drawing the view out of the window."

The look of relief on his mother's face was reward enough for his effort to be cheerful, but he surprised her even more. "I say, Mum, why ought I to thank God that this accident wasn't worse?" he asked. "Anne says He doesn't send troubles, but He doesn't often stop them, either. She says if we didn't come up against some hard things we'd never learn to be tough, or to help other people and that sort of thing. But if I could have been killed, why didn't God let me be? Or buried alive in that hole last week?"

"Goodness gracious! What an enormous question! I'm not sure that I can answer it entirely. I don't think anyone could," said his mother, honestly. "I've a feeling that it's where prayer comes in. No one really understands the power of prayer, but it's pretty certain that people who are prayed for are helped a lot. Of course, I do ask God to take care of you every day of your life. We know that prayers aren't always answered in the way we want them to be, but I'm certain they're always heard."

"I guess that's a good enough answer," Justin told her, with a sudden smile, and added, with a chuckle, "Of course Anne was down the hole, too, so perhaps it was Anne who was worth saving!"

The next week dragged for Justin, but he kept his promise and tried very hard not to grumble or to make more work for old Mrs Lott than he could help. He was allowed downstairs for an hour or two every day, and explored the big bookcase in the stuffy little sitting-room. There were not many books to his taste, but he found one called *Prehistoric, Roman, and Saxon Britain*. He carried that one eagerly to the chair by the window. A few weeks ago he would have passed it by as 'boring old history', but now the pages about early warriors, and potters, and herdsmen seemed to come alive for him. He searched through, trying to find any place-names that he knew, and was eager to find drawings of ancient jewels and ornaments.

I could have done a much better project for school if I'd known all this a week or two back, he thought, regretfully.

The next afternoon, when Mrs Lott had got him comfortably settled with his tea on a small tray, and *Prehistoric Britain* propped open on the windowsill, a shadow fell across the book. There, outside the window, was Sandy, clutching an armful of magazines and a yo-yo.

"Come in!" cried Justin. "Go and knock on the door. Mrs Lott's in the kitchen; she'll let you in. I expected you days ago."

He didn't give Sandy time to be awkward. "Have one of these buns old Lottie makes," he offered, when

Sandy had joined him. "She's a smashing cook, which helps things a lot. Any news about our hole? No one has much time to come and tell me anything."

"Not your hole specially," said Sandy, reaching out for a bun, "but did you hear on the radio this morning that the ground has dropped five feet in a place near Widdens Cross? One long stretch of it, they said, at the corner of a field, and a cow fell down and had to be rescued. Dad said he wondered if there were any more old places, or passages underground. They might have been forgotten for ages, but the winter rains could have made their roofs cave in at last."

Justin's eyes brightened. "There might be other space for us to find when I'm better," he said. "All of you, and Anne as well, might help me prowl round next summer holidays. You'll have finished digging your mine and making your rockery by then."

Sandy couldn't stay long because his own tea was waiting, but just before he went he said, casually, "Have you heard about the thing our school's doing for Open Day? We're putting on a set of tableaux of special things that have happened in this bit of Kent from Roman times till now. Sir has knocked up a great wooden frame, and my form is painting a background of the North Downs."

"Anne said something about it when she came, but I had such a bad head that day that I didn't really listen," Justin admitted. "She said something about houses coming and going, and I got a bit muddled."

"Sounds like an earthquake," Sandy chuckled. "What she meant was that we've got slits in the background, very cunning ones, where we can slip in bits showing other things. A wattle hut, or a castle, or an oast house or two, according to the date. You'll jolly well have to come and see, becuse our head has asked Mr Cassidy if we can borrow that old propeller you found for the Great War bit."

Justin sat up straight for the first time without hurting himself. "I'll come even if I have to make you carry me!" he cried. "I want to keep an eye on that propeller. Mr Priddy didn't think it would count as treasure, so they might at least let me have the broken bit. I suppose," he added, his old impish grin coming back again, "I suppose the rabbits really ought to be given it. After all, they started the hole!"

CHAPTER NINE

RACE AGAINST TIME

Justin felt absolutely wonderful when at last he was home for good, and allowed to get up for breakfast. He longed for the weekend when all his friends would not be at school, because it was rather lonely wandering around by himself.

But when Saturday did come it seemed as though he was going to have a rather solitary day, after all. Mum was on duty again that day, and every one of his friends was going to cheer on their chosen team at an away match.

"We're going into town on the early bus, and joining the special train," Sandy told him on Friday night. "All the fellows from your school, and half the schools in the county will be going, as well; even Carol's coming! Can't you possibly be with us? I'm sure you're well enough."

"Not if someone thumped me, or pushed me back against a rail, Mum says. Besides, I'd just be grousing to myself because it'll be ages before I can play again," Justin said, gloomily. "I haven't tried running, yet. I'm half scared to, in case it hurts again."

So it happened that Justin wandered into the brightness of Saturday morning with his hands in his pockets, wondering what to do with himself till it was time to go to Mrs Lott's for dinner.

He went and looked at his bicycle, and was delighted to see that it was polished and clean. Sandy had seen to that, but riding was forbidden to him for a while so he shut the shed door and went out into the road. The tooting of a horn made him look up. A green van slowed, and stopped beside him.

"Nice to see you out!" said a voice, and there was Tom Stubbs, older brother of one of his school friends. "Want a lift anywhere?" he added, opening the door. "I'm going round by Tyler's Gate. Like me to put you down at the cross-roads—then you could stroll back home. Nice, gentle exercise!"

Justin was delighted, and not a little flattered that Tom had noticed him. He climbed in and settled back to enjoy the short drive, thinking how green everything had become in the short time since he had gone into hospital.

"Not going to the football match?" said Tom. "I suppose you'd cheer yourself silly and start jumping up and down, and that might not be too good for the old spine. If you're back home by twelve, though, you could cheer the team as the train goes through the level-crossing. My young brother's got a scarf about twenty feet long! I guess he'll be waving it out of the window all the way."

"By twelve! I'll be back ages before that. Thanks for a jolly good idea," said Justin. "I'll cheer them on if I can't do anything else."

All too soon Tom stopped at the cross-roads and left Justin standing on the grass bank, looking after the green van. He thought of the road back home, and decided it was rather plain and ordinary. Surely there was something more adventurous he could do in the long gap which stretched ahead till twelve o'clock.

He went to lean on a field gate and rack his brains

for ideas. The field sloped down towards the flat land across which the railway ran, and away to his left he could see the line of woodlands which was the hazel coppice beside their hole.

Further down that gentle slope, beyond the woods, he could see the spire of Widdens church. Looking the other way he could see in the distance the scatter of red roofs that was his own village. It was all very quiet, and there was not even a lark singing. The field beyond him, greening over with young wheat, looked as empty as the sky. Then a train appeared, like a small toy on the distant line, the only moving thing in the wide landscape.

Suddenly an idea came to Justin which seemed absolutely perfect. He climbed the gate and sat on the top a moment, thinking. If he kept along by the hedge that divided the fields, so as not to tread on the wheat, he could make his way to the railway line. All down hill and easy going, he told himself. Beside the high railway bank there was a beaten path he knew. Sandy and Pete had walked along it all the way to the next town, Pete had boasted one day. It would fill up the morning nicely to stroll along by the bank and arrive at the level-crossing in time for twelve o'clock.

The field was exceedingly muddy. Justin soon had to stop and find sharp flints to push some of the clinging mud off his shoes because it made for slow going. Lots of flints here, he thought, and wished the wheat was not growing. If it wasn't so high he could have ranged across the plough looking for puddy stones instead of keeping by the hedge.

Then he had a surprise. Right ahead of him there was a sudden dip in the ground. It looked as though a narrow slice of the field had dropped about three feet.

It was still smooth and green, but he looked down on it from a miniature cliff.

I wonder however they cut the corn that grows in a ditch like that, thought Justin, and then he remembered the scrap of conversation with Sandy. Hadn't he said that some ground had dropped near Widdens? This couldn't be the place, though, because Sandy had said that a cow had fallen down, and one didn't have cows in a wheat field.

Cautiously he skirted round the edge of the fallen earth, and went on towards the railway wondering if the 'ditch' was a fresh one, and if the farmer knew about it yet. He had almost reached the rails when he saw another scar which had cut through the wheat. It was shallower than the first, and not so green. In fact, it was a wonderful jumble of earth and flints, too good to pass unsearched.

Ignoring the fact that it was so soft that both his shoes were caked all over, Justin prowled round the edge of it. He turned over stones, trying not to notice that his back was beginning to ache just a bit. And then he saw it! Quite close to his left foot lay a puddy stone, with the fossil mark clear and strong.

"Wow! What a beauty!" exclaimed Justin, with delight, crouching down to prise it from the earth with eager fingers. For several minutes he stayed there, rubbing the mud off it and seeing how the tiny dents formed a pattern of surprising beauty.

Not a cross this time, he thought; more like a halo. I think one of the old shepherds would have kept it for his girl, and not felt that it should go into the chapel.

A quick movement near him made him look up. A young hare was sitting on its hind legs only a few feet away, gazing at him with great brown eyes. Justin drew a quick breath of pleasure, but the surprise made him move slightly and in a second the hare was gone. Justin twisted to watch it loping away along the field edge, and it was at that moment he realised with a shock that he was looking right through the railway bank. The earth of the embankment was a good two feet lower just opposite him, and for several yards the rails were in the air with sleepers dangling.

For a moment he stared in disbelief. Below the rails, framed by the sides of a wide gap, he could see a field with sheep, and beyond that the sea.

"But a train passed," he said, aloud, in a choked kind of whisper. "It couldn't have been like this then!"

As though in answer to his thought there was a shuddering of the earth below the rails, and a scatter of stones rolled down the bank. A couple of seconds later Justin's view of the sea was twice as big.

He stood up with a horrible dread gripping him. If another train came by and hit that gap there would be a most ghastly accident.

Suddenly he remembered what he had come that way for. Finding the puddy stone had put everything else out of his mind for the moment, but now it came back with terrible force—the football train! In twenty minutes it would come roaring by.

Scrambling on to the worn track beside the embankment, Justin began to run. The effort made twinges of pain shoot up his spine, but to begin with he scarcely noticed them. His one thought was to get to the level-crossing. The man in the little box beside the gate would have a telephone.

He had not realised how far it was. He could see

the trees that stood beside the Ridetts' house, and a blur of buildings near them, but it seemed a terribly long way away, hazy in the spring sunshine. After a few minutes of trotting with all the speed he could muster, the pain in his back began to get really bad. He found that he was still clutching the stone he had picked up, and somehow the feel of it gripped in his palm gave him comfort. It did something else, too. It reminded him of those other stones in the dim little chapel, and how Mr Cassidy had called them 'steps to God'.

He stumbled, and found his footing again, and began praying in little, gasping sentences. "Please, God—please, God—help me to save the train—Sandy's on it, and all the others—please don't let my back hurt so much that I stop."

Something Anne had said flickered through his mind. "Queen Bertha must have been a wonderful stayer. She just kept on, however hard things were, till she had built her church and people began to turn to God."

A stayer! Perhaps that was what was asked of him now. He just had to beat the pain and the distance, somehow, because people needed him. He was forced to walk for a few moments from sheer lack of breath, and as he walked Justin suddenly knew the answer to something which had always puzzled him. When Mum took him to church at Easter he had always wondered why Jesus allowed Himself to be crucified. Justin was sure He could have got out of it quite easily by making friends with the High Priest. But He just had to go on with it because there were people who needed saving, people who had to see that God's way wasn't the High Priest's way.

"Help me now," Justin prayed. "Help me after this to be one of the people who belong to You."

The last hundred yards were agony because his chest hurt badly as well as his back.

Justin could see the dim figure of the crossing keeper beyond the window of his little box, and he waved as he stumbled on. But the man was looking away down the line. The gates were open, and cars streamed through, anxious to get on their way before the road was closed to let the football special through. There was a wire fence to squeeze between, and then another before Justin gained the road, and then the steps up to the box were right ahead.

He tried to shout, but his mouth was dry, and now the man had strolled across to look out of the far window. It was another five minutes before he needed to close the gates again, and the mid-day up-train was running late. He turned suddenly as a gasping sound came from the door behind him. A boy with staring eyes and a chalk-white face was dragging himself up the last step.

"What!" began the man. "What the—— Are you ill?"

Justin clutched the door handle and his words came hoarsely but very urgent. "The earth's caved in under the line back there—the rails are hanging in the air—you—must—stop the football train!"

For one second the crossing keeper suspected a hoax, but changed his mind speedily as Justin gasped out another word, "Telephone", and collapsed on the floor.

Far down the line, with striped scarves and rattles waving from its windows, the special pulled out of

Widdens Junction.

"Now it's a through train all the way!" chanted Pete, and Sandy jockeyed for a position nearer the window.

"Don't we stop at Queenbridge, and all the little places?" asked a small boy at his elbow and Sandy assured him that they didn't.

But two minutes later, as Queenbridge Halt came into view they felt the train slowing. "Well I'm blowed," said Sandy. "I suppose they've had to stop to pick up some V.I.P. or other."

They little guessed that the football special had stopped altogether.

CHAPTER TEN

ANNE OF THE GOLDEN NECKLET

Suddenly the tiny hamlet of Widdens, the level-crossing, and Justin himself were on everybody's tongue.

"Football train saved by minutes!" said a notice outside the newspaper shop, and Anne bought a copy of the 'local' because her friends were in it.

For a day or two Justin was too uncomfortable to join in the general excitement, or to be among the crowds of people who trooped to see the great rift which now ran right down the field, and beyond. They went to watch the men who worked furiously to build a new and firm foundation under that part of the old branch railway line.

It was rest in bed again for Justin, though the doctor assured him that the pain would go away, and that he would be as good as new by mid-summer. This time it was all so much easier to bear.

"It's worth while because nobody was hurt," he told himself each time a twinge caught him when he moved. This time, too, he had more company. Mrs Ridett had been called by the crossing keeper, who saw her in her garden. She had got help to carry Justin indoors, and there he remained. She insisted that it was in their house he should be nursed till he was about again, so that his mother could carry on with her work and have much less worry; and old Mrs Lott would have no bother at all.

It meant, too, that as soon as school was over each day there would be Sandy or Carol, Pete, Mark or small Kate coming to talk to him, and bringing their guinea-pigs to visit.

Mrs Ridett spoiled him all she knew how. "I could have lost my boys, and Carol, too, if there had been a crash," she kept telling his mother, who was afraid Justin might take too much advantage of the situation.

But Justin had been doing a lot of sober thinking, and was more inclined to thank God that he had been used in a wonderful way and helped to keep running to the end. He felt very strongly that God had called him to be of service, and because of that he didn't regard himself as a hero.

He had had a long talk with Mrs Ridett, too, and she had explained to him carefully something he had never understood before.

"None of us can be really happy, or feel at peace with God," she said, "unless we realise that Jesus Christ is our Saviour. If we ask Him to come into our lives and help us to do good things instead of bad things day by day, He has promised that He will do it, and never, never leave us. The word 'Saviour' puzzles some people," she went on. "It means that when Jesus died on the cross He was bearing the punishment for the sins of the whole world. God has promised to forgive everyone who is truly sorry for the bad things they have done, all because of what Jesus did for us so long ago."

Justin hadn't said much at the time, but when Mrs Ridett cam into his room to say good-night he reached out and caught her hand.

"I did what you said," he told her. "I asked God to

forgive me for Jesus' sake for everything bad I've done, and to help me be the sort of boy Jesus wants. I didn't hear any kind of answer, or see anything special, but I've got a feeling deep down that He will."

"I know He will!" said Mrs Ridett, gladly, as she switched out the light.

Of course, Justin was deeply interested in all the talk about 'Widdens Rift'. It was caused by old, forgotten mine workings which went right out under the sea, geologists said. Down in the depths of the earth there had been some movement which had made the field above sink in a long line. "But what about our chapel?" Justin asked Anne when she came one evening, saying she had less homework than usual.

"Mr Cassidy thinks it's part of the same 'rift', our hole," she told him. "He thinks it probably wasn't rabbits or a badger digging that started it. In fact, there's a crack right across the chapel floor now, and the hole has a proper fence round it with a big red notice saying 'Danger'."

"So we won't be able to go down again?" asked Justin, disappointed.

" 'fraid not. Even the diggers are keeping out of it now."

Anne went to lean out of the window in answer to a shout from Pete. "They're larking about down there," she told Justin. "Kate is in the wheelbarrow. They'll tip her out if they're not careful!" Justin sighed. "Silly chumps!" he said, and wished he was out in the sun with them. Anne went on watching, and laughing at the antics down below, till Justin made her forget everything else and listen to him with joy.

"You know," he said soberly, "finding that small

chapel, and those puddy stones on the altar, and hearing about Queen Bertha, made my history lessons come alive. I've always been so bored with history and wondered what good it was, anyway; but now I feel different.

"Those old people seem to speak to us, somehow, in the things they left behind. Queen Bertha—she had a tough job to do for God, and the things she left seem to say that God helped her, and that He'll help us if we do our part. You know, I found a puddy stone just before I saw right through that railway bank—I'm sure it wasn't an accident that it was there. God wanted me to stop, and look, so that I should notice the gap and save the train."

"So you really do believe? You really know He's here with us all the time?" Anne's grey eyes were full of happiness, and her face had quite a flush, which wasn't just the sun coming through the window.

Justin nodded. "What's more," he said, "just like I'm reading everything I can find about Romans and Saxons, so I'm wanting to read about Jesus. I'm not finding the Bible boring any longer, either. In fact," he added, "Sandy's talked me into coming with them on Sunday mornings when I can get around again. He says I can give out the hymns and keep the small kids in order, to begin with, till I've learned enough to really help."

"Jolly good for you!" said Anne, fervently. "When you can ride again you might like to come to the church youth group in Hammersly. They've got quite a big one, and they do all sorts of things. Sandy says he'll come, and Carol, so Mother won't mind me going all that way if I'm with a crowd. I believe each one of us has got to be a 'step to God' for someone else by helping them to know about Him. For you, the tiddlers in the Sunday school could be a start."

It was the next afternoon when Sandy arrived with some news which gave Justin plenty to think about. "You've just got to be around on your feet by the time we have Open Day at our school," he announced. "We're really going to town this time! Because of all the fluff about 'Widdens Rift', Sir is making a much bigger thing of those tableaux. He's making more of a pageant of it, and he's having a bit about Queen Bertha as well as the Roman bits. Then he's got a much later piece about pilgrims going through Widdens on their way to Canterbury."

"Sounds jolly good," said Justin. "I wish it was at my school. Anne goes to yours, doesn't she? You said once that she wasn't really a school friend, not till she helped you with the quarry."

"Didn't know her at all till she came to her Aunt Madge. There are such masses of us now from all the villages round. I guess Anne will be in the crowd that's making costumes," Sandy said. Then he had a bright idea. "You're good with your hands, and jolly good at drawing and making models, so your mum says. You'll be sitting up in bed in a day or two, and bored to tears. How would you like to make lots of strings of beads, and cut out scallop shell shapes, and little spiky 'martyr's crowns'?"

"Whatever for?" asked Justin, not sure if Sandy was pulling his leg.

"For the pilgrims—pedlars are to have them on trays hung round their necks, souvenirs to sell to the people to remind them of Thomas Becket. Sir says he wants pedlars to stand on the edge of the stage offering things to the pilgrims passing by. He said anyone who wanted to could make some things for the trays at home. I'm sure he wouldn't mind if you helped, because there were such a lot of us on that wretched football train."

So that was how Justin found himself with plenty to do while he waited for the doctor to let him be up and about. With a tray on his knees, and cardboard, glue, scissors and sticky tape, he made enough 'souvenirs' to satisfy a regiment of pilgrims.

He begged some baking foil from Mrs Ridett and fashioned some really splendid clasps and brooches for the Saxon chieftains, too. The ideas for those he found in Mr Lott's book, which the old man gladly lent him.

At last the day came when he was downstairs and joining in a noisy game with The Level-crossing Kids. They took him out to show him proudly that at last they had finished the little rockery and its paved 'courtyard'. The little pond was in place, but not yet filled, and Justin watched while Mark proudly organised a bucket procession to and from the kitchen, slopping water as they went. By the next week they hoped to have goldfish swimming.

Sitting there in the sun, and seeing the bluebells all out by the hedge, Justin thought what a lot had happened since the first evening when he strolled by to see what they were all doing. The level-crossing gates closed with a clang, and as he looked across and saw the cars stopping to wait for the train he knew that he had changed a lot since that day. He was a 'new person'.

It was three weeks later that the result of all Justin's hard work was seen at the school's Open Day.

Justin, while he sat up in bed carefully cutting and making the pilgrim 'souvenirs' had expected to be one of the audience looking on at the pageant. He just hoped he would get a seat where it was possible to see everything.

But the day after he had watched the Ridetts fill their pool he had gone back to his own home, and there he found a letter waiting for him. Would he like to actually take part in the pageant? Sandy's headmaster asked. They felt, he said, that though Justin went to another school he was so much part of the village, and they all owed him a great deal for stopping the football train. It would be nice if he could share in their remembrance of village history. There would only be a 'crowd' part for him, he explained, but they needed plenty of extras in the scene where Queen Bertha led the villagers to meet Augustine.

"Look, Mum! Isn't this great!" Justin pushed the letter across the table to where his mother was trying to add up her weekly accounts. She looked up, happy to hear the eagerness in his voice which told that he was feeling really well again.

"That's splendid!" she exclaimed. "I think it shows they really liked all these things you made. What part is Anne taking in all this? She's in it, surely?"

"Making costumes, I think Sandy said. I really don't know," Justin admitted. "I know Sandy is a Roman soldier, and Pete is just going to be a local boy dressed in skins. Kate and Mark aren't in it, anyway, because they're in the junior school. They're in the choir that sings before the thing really starts."

And that was all he knew until he turned up, rather

shyly, at a rehearsal, glad to have Sandy and Carol to pilot him through an unfamiliar building. Soon he had discarded his own blazer and grey trousers for a rough tunic of brown sacking, with a twist of straw rope round his waist.

"You'd better have this long, crooked stick," said the stage manager. "You're supposed to be a shepherd. We may manage to get a decent model of a lamb for you to carry on the night, but, anyway, the stick will give you something to do with your hands."

A shepherd! thought Justin. Well, I know one thing; I'm going to take my puddy stone with me. A real shepherd of that time could have found just the same stone if a plough turned it up, or rabbits kicked it out.

The crowded on to the stage, to be moved here and there by a master, and all of them turned to see Queen Bertha enter with her attendant maidens. To Justin's joy it was Anne—Anne very dignified and royal, with her straw-coloured plaits hanging forward over her shoulders, much lengthened with artificial hair.

She gave him a quirky smile as she went by, and Justin had a feeling that she probably had something to do with him being there at all.

At last the evening came when the school assembly hall was crowded with parents and friends. By that time Justin had lost the feeling of strangeness, and from his place by the edge of the stage he could peep through a tiny gap in the curtains and see so many faces that he knew. They all looked friendly and expectant.

The voices of the junior school choir came strongly from their screened place behind the piano. "And did those feet in ancient time, walk upon England's mountains green." Just right, thought Justin, and then someone touched him on the arm. It was Anne, with her face positively radiant. She unclasped from her neck a slender band with heartshaped decorations, a collar of gold.

"The torque!" exclaimed Justin, only just remembering to whisper.

"A copy," whispered Anne. "Mr Cassidy gave it to me. Isn't he a darling? It's made of a modern alloy that can look like gold. He got a jeweller to make it!"

She clasped it back again round her neck, and as she caught up her heavy robe and moved away Justin guessed that this was a day Anne would remember all her life.

And so shall I, he thought, when just a little later his turn came to move on to the stage. From the wings opposite walked the sturdy figure of a monk, with two others close behind him. One carried a tall cross, and as Bertha came forward to meet Augustine she knelt a moment in homage.

With all the other 'villagers' Justin also sank on his knees. He laid his crook on the ground, and clasped his model lamb gently as though it had been a small, living animal. He was clasping something else too, for in the palm of his right hand he held the puddy stone.

As he looked up at the cross held high, he knew that all his life he must follow where that symbol led.